COPING:

ISSUES OF EMOTIONAL LIVING
IN AN AGE OF STRESS
FOR CLERGY AND RELIGIOUS

COPING:

ISSUES OF EMOTIONAL LIVING IN AN AGE OF STRESS FOR CLERGY AND RELIGIOUS

THE FIRST BOSTON PSYCHOTHEOLOGICAL SYMPOSIUM

By

BERNARD J. BUSH
THOMAS A. KANE
PHILOMENA AGUDO
RICHARD J. GILMARTIN

With a Foreword by
ANNA POLCINO, M.D.

Founder and Psychiatric Director, House of Affirmation

Instructor in Psychiatry,
University of Massachusetts Medical School

AFFIRMATION BOOKS
WHITINSVILLE, MASSACHUSETTS, U.S.A.

PUBLISHED WITH ECCLESIASTICAL PERMISSION

Printed by Mercantile Printing Company, Worcester, Mass.
United States of America

To

Present and former residents
of the House of Affirmation
with love and gratitude

AUTHORS

Reverend Thomas A. Kane, Ph.D., D.P.S.

Richard J. Gilmartin, M.A., C.A.G.S.

Sister Philomena Agudo, F.M.M., M.A., Ph.D.

Reverend Bernard J. Bush, S.J., M.A., Th.M.

Contents

Foreword

To Fall in Love with God
is the greatest
of all romances!

To Seek Him
is the greatest
of all adventures!

To Find Him
is the greatest
human achievement!

— Fr. M. Raphael Simon, O.C.S.O., M.D.

"To fall in love with God, to seek Him, to find Him," is indeed, a lifetime quest. It is a quest in which the anxieties, griefs, joys and hopes of each person are intimately bound with the anxieties, griefs, joys and hopes of other persons. For we do not cope with the challenges of life in a vacuum. Our lives are made up of interpersonal relationships — woman to woman, man to man, woman to man, man to woman.

The Fathers of Vatican II were not unaware of the changed and changing conditions of our historical period; reference is made to technology which is fast transforming the face of the earth, to the advances made in biochemistry and biogenetics, psychology, the behavioral and social sciences for improving self-knowledge and the life of social groups. They note, "recent psychological research explains human activity more profoundly." A similar concern is found in the *Decree on the Appropriate Renewal of the Religious Life,* "the manner of living, praying and working should be suitably adapted to the physical and psychological conditions of today's religious . . . to the needs of the apostolate, the requirements of a given culture."

There is no doubt that a psychotheological approach to living this quest for God is evident in the Vatican II considerations. In reality, the Church from all times has realized the importance of mental and physical health and its relationship to the supernatural or the spiritual dimension of a person. This recurrent theme is found in the prayers of the liturgy where the Church continually prays for health of mind and body.

The expression "psychotheological community" implies a common quest for communion with God and with man. It informs the religious professional of the fact that personhood can only be realized in community where unity is respectful of the diverse gifts of its members. The establishment of interpersonal relationships constitutes the first step in building community. While being present to and sharing with one another, all members contribute to the community while each person remains a unique individual; it is the unitive bond of common religious values, the friendliness of the community members that serve to bring out and to enrich what is uniquely true of each individual.

Such a psychotheological approach and psychotheological community have been developed at the House of Affirmation so that the religious professional who has lived for years in an unhappy state of neurotic conflict can re-learn healthier ways of coping and so integrate the physical, psychological and spiritual dimensions of his personality.

So it is with great joy that the House of Affirmation makes available in print one of its seminars. It is with a sense of solidarity that "charity urges us" to share our valuable experiences and insights with other concerned persons who will read and reflect on this publication of COPING: ISSUES OF EMOTIONAL LIVING IN AN AGE OF STRESS FOR CLERGY AND RELIGIOUS.

Sister Anna Polcino, S.C.M.M., M.D.
Founder and Psychiatric Director of House of Affirmation
Instructor in Psychiatry
University of Massachusetts
Medical School

Preface

The four essays in this volume are the result of a symposium given at Aquinas Junior College, Newton, Massachusetts, on October 4, 1975. The symposium was sponsored by the House of Affirmation, International Therapeutic Center for Clergy and Religious. The response to the symposium was far beyond our expectations, as 700 clergy, religious and lay persons attended where we had originally planned for about 150. Since then we have had numerous requests for copies of the presentations. So we decided to offer the talks in printed form. We have tried as much as possible to keep the colloquial style and informality which characterized the day itself. Some of the fun we had, the humorous asides, the interchanges between the speaker and the panel during the presentations, and references to local happenings have had to be omitted in the interest of the printed rather than the spoken word. However, we feel that enough of the flavor has been retained to give the reader an informative and relaxing experience.

The House of Affirmation was founded in 1970 by Sister Anna Polcino, S.C.M.M., M.D., as a non-residential consulting center for clergy and religious in Worcester, Massachusetts. On October 1, 1973, a residential treatment center was opened in Whitinsville, Massachusetts, and a year later a non-resident satellite office was opened in Boston. Just three days before the symposium another office was opened in Birmingham, England. These expansions have been made in response to the expressed need for our services.

The primary focus of the ministry of the House of Affirmation is the treatment of mental and emotional problems of religious professionals in a therapeutic community setting. However, our stated goals are service, education, and research. It is in fulfillment of the educational goal that workshops such as this one on coping are offered.

Perhaps the most characteristic feature of the staff of the House of Affirmation is a deep conviction shared by all that we are dedicated to a unique mission of service to the Church. That said, in almost every other respect we are as diverse as the Church itself. Our staff embraces the whole spectrum of humanity: diocesan clergy, religious of nine different orders, lay men and women, married, single and widowed. We come from different nations, cultures and regions. Our educational backgrounds, psychological and theological education and personalities are widely varied. It is out of this context that we have formed a very intense bond of love, support, caring and healing that is our therapeutic community. We have a deep faith and trust in God whose help we seek and depend upon constantly to supply for our deficiencies.

We call our approach psychotheological. In practice the word means that we blend elements of many schools of theology and psychology. We have found that much of the practice of humanistic psychology fails to appreciate the dimensions of faith and commitment to God, religious values, the transcendent and mysterious (in the spiritual sense), worship, and the need of prayer. Since many religious professionals have distorted beliefs in some of these areas, we feel that the distortions need to be modified as part of the whole treatment program. Much practice of psychology either ignores the person's religious belief system because it is incompetent to handle it, or at worst considers it symptomatic of illness. This is not to deny that there is much truth in the discoveries of psychology and the other behavioral sciences. They have shed much light on what it means to be human. A psychotheological approach, then, searches the sources in the psychological sciences to find the truth they offer toward understanding the inner workings of humanity, and the sources in theology to find the truth of faith concerning God and our relationship to Him and to one another. Our approach, therefore, is one of integration and reconciliation.

Once the general topic of the symposium and points of focus were decided upon, a problem still remained. Exactly what does it mean "to cope"? The word itself seems to have derived from the French *couper*, to strike a blow. It has a military or violent connotation as in *coup d'etat*, and *coup de grace*. From this it has come in our usage to mean adaptive behavior. It still has the overtones of struggle to overcome some obstacle. The new situation or challenge requiring coping may be within ourselves such as illness, feelings, new ideas, etc., or outside ourselves such as persons, values, historical changes, external threats, etc. Thus, for the purposes of this symposium we have chosen a working definition which includes all these elements. Coping is a response of adaptation or adjustment to the stress produced by changing circumstances in one's life situation.

We have chosen four areas from the life situation of religious professionals today which are presently vulnerable to change and very much in flux. They are areas which affect our lives deeply since they touch closely on our identity as religious persons. Changes in these dimensions of living produce feelings of anxiety and confusion which must be faced and coped with successfully if we are going to lead happy lives. The topics we are going to discuss are community, humanity, meaning, and God. The House of Affirmation is in existence because there is much maladaptive and unsuccessful coping. Our hope is that by efforts such as this we will be instrumental in spreading the word of health and healing through affirmation of the person.

A word of thanks is in order to all who contributed to the success of the symposium, and who have supported and encouraged us in this work of writing. I would like to thank the participants for their generosity in risking to present very personal material along with clinical expertise. The entire staff of the House of Affirmation was superb in their support and contributions. Most of the staff and some of their spouses were present at the symposium to handle the details, answer questions, and be available for conversation. Many of our residents, non-residents and former residents were also present to explain our ministry in conversations throughout the day. We have a special appreciation for the graciousness of the Sisters of St. Joseph who made available to us their beautiful facilities at Aquinas Junior College and remained on hand to help with the minor problems that came up. We are grateful to the couple from the emblem company who donated a banner for the occasion. To the Sisters who loaned us tapes of the talks since we did not make any of our own, to the Sister who suggested the title and program, and to the many who helped with printing, typing, mailing, registration, and bookkeeping, we say thank you, for without you it could not have happened. Finally we are grateful to all who attended the October symposium despite competition from celebrations in honor of St. Francis, St. Elizabeth Seton, and the World Series.

Bernard J. Bush, S.J.
Boston, Massachusetts
December 8, 1975
Feast of the Immaculate Conception

The Rev. Dr. Thomas A. Kane is a priest of the Roman Catholic Diocese of Worcester. His undergraduate studies were at St. Edward's University, Austin, Texas; his graduate studies at National University of Mexico, Rutgers University, and St. Bonaventure University; and his postgraduate studies at Boston University and the University of Birmingham, Edgbaston, England. As educator and psychologist, Father Kane is consultant to several Roman Catholic and Protestant groups. He is a frequent lecturer to academic and medical communities. A member of several professional organizations, he is a Wall Street Journal Fellow, 1964, and was awarded the 1972 Chamber of Commerce Outstanding Young Leader Award. Doctor Kane is listed in the 1975 Dictionary of International Biography and was recently elected to the Board of Directors of the National Guild of Catholic Psychiatrists. He is a founder and present Executive Director of House of Affirmation, International Therapeutic Center for Clergy and Religious, in Whitinsville, Massachusetts. He is author of "Who Controls Me?" and "The Healing Touch of Affirmation."

CHAPTER ONE

COPING WITH COMMUNITY
Thomas A. Kane

Good morning.

It occurred to me when Father Bush was doing the introductions that it is quite true what he said about the corporate nature of today's panel: a religious Sister, a religious priest, a married layman, and a diocesan priest. However, the two religious and the married person have chosen a diocesan priest to speak about *community!* I do not know what that means; but same would lend to interesting reflection.

AFFIRMATION

Also in his prefatory remarks, Father Bush explained the origin of the word "coping" and its meaning. Coping is an essential part of affirmation, but not synonymous with affirmation. The word affirmation comes from the Latin *affirmare* and it means to make firm, to give strength to, to make strong.

Affirmation is concerned with being and not primarily with doing. Affirmation is the essence and core of all mature love. The most tender, delicate, indeed, healing touch of affirmation is that I allow the other person to be as he is, immaturity and shortcomings included. I do so not out of fear but out of free choice, and encourage the other to be who he is so that his full potential may be realized.

The best book available on affirmation is ABOUT LOVE by Josef Pieper. I recommend this book to you for careful and reflective reading. Pieper's thesis maintains that affirmation is synonymous with creation. Creating strengthens mankind and compels him to seek truth and exalt the

goodness and beauty of all that is. The psychology of affirmation or creation goes beyond the utilitarianism so often found in the Western world.

The idea of affirmation opens new perspectives not only for individuals but for society in general, and Christian communities in particular. In my book WHO CONTROLS ME? I offer the following reflection: "It is evident from what has been said thus far that there is required much more new and bold thinking if we are to meet the challenge of the future. Affirmation can affect the future; it does not, however, seek to control; it is like the sun upon the rose bringing it to blossom.

Having been affirmed by another and affirming others, I will know and feel who I am; I will have a true identity. I will sense that I am different but acceptable, that I belong in the world but that I am contributing to it and can change it; that there is a unique place for me and that I have a unique contribution, that I can choose freely to do and to love, that I cannot be ultimately destroyed and am confidently open to what is to come."

HEALTH

Having said a few words about affirmation, let us continue our topic on coping with community. But let us do so from the viewpoint of health, not illness. Too often today our stress is on illness and not on health. As a therapist, I often go to "mental health" conferences only to find the agenda filled with topics such as schizophrenia, addiction, neuroses, etc., and I am often at a loss to find any topic on health per se.

Affirmation of human dignity is health. In a healthy community, difference is enrichment presenting the challenge of unity. We go to community to grow in health. Community should mean opportunity for growth, wonder, being who I am and significantly sharing in healthy growth with others.

I believe the Church is that community which has the best potential for mankind to realize its quest for health and community. None of us are going to communities that offer a slow emotional death. Several months ago, I was giving a seminar in England and in the process of being introduced the person announced that this American psychologist would give advice on what to do in a sinking Church. My response had to be honest. Tactfully as I could I advised my listeners that if they believed they were on a sinking ship good psychology would say hurry up and get off! If I believed that the Church was sinking or that ecclesial communities had nothing to say to contemporary values, I, then, would be among the first to swim away. The Church, to me, rich in its tradition, ever fresh in its articulation, offers affirmation — strength, nobility of being, and a creative atmosphere for growth, healing and health. Jesus Christ whose Body is the Church offers us the gift of being affirmed members in love; in His Body we know a new dignity and become thinkers of our thoughts and feelers of our feelings.

HEALING

So we come to community; we share in groups for our own health and for the health of others. We come to community to celebrate the corporate aspects of healing.

Healing is a word so often on the lips of religious professionals nowadays. Rightly so, for healing is what community is all about. But we must have a commonality of definition if we are to have an intelligent reflection today. I would like to share a brief definition of healing with you. I suggest that *healing is a satisfactory response to a crisis made by a group of people, both as individuals and collectively*. This definition contains no specific word barriers. Thus, physicians, nurses, therapists, social workers, clergymen, religious, theologians and most of all other people can relate to it. This proposed definition is based on Paul's letters to the Church at Corinth, the Encyclical on the Mystical Body and the Vatican II Constitution on the Church.

Healing is a response, a satisfactory response, *enough* of a response, to a crisis. In the New Testament the word crisis (krisis) is used frequently and often translated as "judgment." The greatest crisis, the satisfactory judgment, is from the Triumphant One. We must think in these terms if this paper is to make any sense.

Healing is a crisis, a judgment, and an opportunity to respond. We come together in community because of a judgment we have made, of a response we have made, initiated by God, but we are moved by our own free will to come together in a group for healing for ourselves and for others.

I may not belong to your particular group, but whatever healing takes place in your group does affect me. I believe this to be ontologically true. It is not just a pious sentiment. Review the current literature in psychology and psychiatry and we see much being written about the corporate nature of healing, of community healing. Our Christian understanding of the Mystical Body hits at the very essence of what the *scientiae humanae* seemingly are just discovering.

AUTHORITY

When we come to the issue of coping, again and again we are speaking about occupational stress or organizational stress that comes about by being a group of people gathered for our own healing, the healing of one another, the healing of the people we serve, and the people we enable to be healers in an affirming community. In a sense, we can say the healer is a person of authority. All of us have the potential, within the healing community, to be authorities in the true sense of the word "authority." A designer, a developer, an enabler . . . try to think in these simple terms for they teach us most about the essence of true authority. What does it mean to be the author of a book? Basically, it means to be an originator, a designer, one who develops and brings out the creativity of meaning. Think about this in your own terms, i.e., the authority you have in terms of affirming relationships in community.

Persons with structured positions of authority must meditate often upon these words. Authority is not power over people. Authority, a true authority, is one who enables, develops, helps design the possibility for the actualization of the potential of the persons entrusted to their pastoral care; this is true of planned as well as emergent leadership.

Thus, we have briefly seen the need to reflect on affirmation, health and healing if coping with community is to be meaningful. Now, I would like to consider seven more psychological factors if there is to be effective identity-fulfilling communal response to the Gospel living. All of these factors make for stable living and successful coping.

RESPONSIBILITY

Effective community living necessarily means that each individual must have a sense of responsibility toward the group as a whole. Somehow the group must work out clearly what this kind of responsibility means. Community cannot exist where people will not speak about and grow toward a clear understanding of individual and corporate responsibility. Healthy and affirming relationships between persons are built upon inescapable and necessary responsibilities. Community should offer a participating experience and this does not mean freedom from responsibility. Freedom does not exist where there is only chaos. Freedom is never synonymous with chaos. Freedom exists within limits. Each community must struggle with understanding of its own limits. Community offers the opportunity to conform as well as to differ. Community means that dialogue exists in the corporate understanding of a clearly marked identity.

Community must offer the opportunity to search for and find stable identification and ideals. Community must allow the opportunity for each of us to ask: What is life all about? What can I receive from life? What can I offer to life? How can I be part of this community and the world? Eventually such integration helps us not only to be concerned about ourselves, but about others, to be tolerant, to be able to be unique individuals, to be ourselves as one in community while still feeling we have our own life to lead. To achieve this psychological maturity, the conflict between the reality of external and internal standards must be resolved without sacrificing completely either our satisfaction for wishes and needs or ethical ideals. The wish or wishes of each individual in community cannot always be directly gratified or continually repressed; they can be achieved indirectly through sublimations and accomplishments.

One knows and feels that he is part of community where shared learning and working together is really happening. Practically speaking, we must realize that in the process of developing a sense of communal responsibility some persons will have more ability to respond than others, some will have less. It is out of loving and being loved that we will want to become part of any community or remain within any community. By experiencing frustration and by experiencing the satisfaction of independent activity, each individual not only tests his own adequacy but learns to deal with the real world instead of one of imagination. Let us stop dealing with the world of imagination in regard to speaking about religious communities. Struggle is part of life. The growth in responsibility is part of what we are talking about this morning as one of the primary constituencies of what community is all about.

That community which pastorally cares for its members will not allow an individual to test himself or herself beyond one's capacity instead of working toward achievable goals. What do I mean by that declarative? I mean that if we are pastorally caring for one another in community, then we will not allow certain members to test themselves beyond what their resources are as we know them to be within the community. There is a delicate balance needed here.

In the past, for example, if we found a Sister who controlled the community by her anger, we would transfer her from house to house, only to find that she is now not present at St. John's, but at St. Mary's where she is displaying the same behavior. Or, if we had a priest who had a problem with alcohol, who was an alcoholic, we transferred him from parish to parish. We chose to ignore our responsibility toward healing. What seems obvious at times is that which I see clinically as most obviously ignored by many communities today. We speak of accountability but we ignore it. We speak about limits and we choose not to establish or articulate limits because it is a dangerous position. To allow any member of a community to take on inappropriate responsibility makes maturity not a stable achievement, but a tenuously accomplished and therefore easily lost frightening task.

LIMITS

Limit need not be an oppressive word. A community with an understanding of the ministry of pastoral care of its own members will promote discussion and realization of limits while at the same time allowing for emotional growth. Members will feel understood. The community will encourage flexibility while creating an atmosphere of adequacy and stability. The awareness of responsibility of the individual toward community and community toward the individual creates a security that serves to absorb the temporary periods of anxiety which any individual within the community may sustain. This awareness of process that enters into community life is what maintains community during inevitable periods of anger or disagreement.

ANGER

This leads us to an immediate awareness of another psychological factor necessary for successful coping with community. Each community must develop the capability of the community as a whole and each of its members to allow and accept expressions of anger. We have come together in community from different backgrounds and each possessing individual personality differences. It is inevitable that conflict will occur and anger arise. We have to give up the idea that there is any such thing as a perfect priest, or a perfect religious, or a perfect community.

Obviously we know anger occurs. Not talking to community members or the cold shoulder pattern is a common way of expressing anger; it appears also to be a destructive expression. There are creative ways of expressing and accepting anger in community that will not destroy individuals or the group as a whole. We must give up the tendency to suffer too much. Although the expression of anger needs to be allowed, this does not mean that the origin of the anger should not be actively explored by the group. Far too often anger is used as a psychological tool to manipulate the community or one another. This sort of testing must be examined for what it really is. One never allows anger to obscure examining the consequences of action. An example that illustrates this point can be found in the individual who "for the sake of peace and harmony" avoids all possible areas of conflict, all anger, even sacrifices principles which should be asserted. I hate that "peace and harmony" cliché because it does so much damage to real peace and authentic harmony. When we know there is no peace and no harmony, let us deal with reality and not play games.

Anger is not a reason, however, to obscure facing each member of the community with what the reality is. If anger is only one aspect of reality and not a threat to it, one does not allow any member of the group to use anger for the purpose of playing on the guilt of others or playing the game — also another cliché — "who takes the blame this time?" When one tries to ignore or escape from the inevitable differences of opinion or of interest, one does so at the price of becoming submissive to others and at the price of ignoring or escaping from one's own sense of individuality and dignity. Without the expression of anger, without the expression of resentment, it is impossible for community members to know each other, and really to meet each other's important and realistic needs. It too often means in a community where the feelings are not being expressed that there exist unresolved and unhealthy dependency struggles, rather than a mutual acceptance of realistic and shared needs and ability.

I think I speak to the experience of many here when I say that for too long within a community we have expected ourselves not to be angry. What I am saying is that it is a healthy sign that you get angry and that you can express it within a community, and that the community does not reject you because you have gotten angry.

But the community too must take on a sense of responsibility toward anger and not allow us or any other member in the group to manipulate the community by our anger. And if we have inevitable situations of discord within the group and within the community, then maturely we have to assess the expression of anger. How many of us will be helped in our growth and development if someone says, "really, you over-reacted, your anger is out of proportion to the situation."! That is a real help. Such is healing for that person, rather than allowing unresolved smoldering that goes on and on and on.

DEPENDENCY

Another psychological factor in coping with community is that individuals living together try to create an atmosphere where there is mutual fulfillment of normal dependency needs. Such an atmosphere allows us to feel relaxed within the community and we experience sufficient emotional security from the group. Thus, we are free to express honest feelings and needs. When the expression of one's feelings and thoughts is accepted, not necessarily agreed with, on a realistic level, then each person within the community will become a more effective adult.

You notice that I say "normal dependency." I do not believe anyone of us can be fully mature or can think about mature life-styles if our dependency needs are not somewhat fulfilled. What I am saying is that we must significantly feel that we are free to say to the community members, "I need you." Of course, some members will be more intimate than others. Too often religious have said, "I need no one." Living in isolation and speaking frequently of community, many have lived and still live without knowing the fulfillment of meaningful communication. There must be mutual identification, mutual awareness of our dependency on each other as fellow human beings.

If community members have an accurate awareness of the strengths and weaknesses of one another, then expectations will be based on supportive and realistic appraisals of who each person is, can be and can do. There will be no magical formulas of perfect success or no fears of total failure. Adaptation to any situation is always a relative matter. Each of us succeeds to a certain degree and each of us fails to a certain degree. It is the achievement of more successes than failures which casts the balance on the side of good mental health.

The fulfillment of our normal dependency needs is, in part, why we come to community. Before we can be fully and maturely independent we must have felt a healthy experience of dependency. I am not speaking here in the construct of thoughts of Freudian terminology where we keep ourselves as children, or that we infantile ourselves with a superior figure. I am stating that to be a mature adult I need a group, a community, upon which I can depend. I need that kind of support. I need that kind of acceptance. I need the community to reflect my own goodness back to me and take delight in it. The community that denies and does not affirm the goodness of its members is on an inevitable path of self-destruction.

Each person has good days and bad days. Most community members are able to be effective adults most of the time. From time to time members will have feelings of doubt and inadequacy about oneself and one's group. Growth comes when the community allows us to be intimately dependent. Then doubts, feelings of uncertainty, feelings of inadequacy, can be expressed and significant others in the community can help us explore the causes and meanings of such internalized conflicts. There is no pushing of the panic button but an opportunity for achieving personality growth and healing. When such health is present in a community, we see little adaptation to the behavior of the luxury of depression. Having said this, we are mindful that clinical depression exists for some individuals and these depressive reactions date back to early childhood. The pastorally concerned community will offer professional assistance for such a person and not penalize the person for a dynamic outside the realm of personal responsibility.

SELF-SUFFICIENCY

Healthy coping in community will necessarily mean that there must exist a level of self-sufficiency for each community member. We have already touched upon this matter in previous paragraphs. The community can help each person to cope with self-sufficiency by dialoguing to create an atmosphere where rivalry is inappropriate rather than allowing rivalry to be part of the unspoken structure.

Self-sufficiency will allow for multiple approaches to the same issue yet all knowing and feeling that the common good is of the essence to any communal living and/ or endeavor. Polarization need not be the by-product of self-sufficient behavior. Self-sufficiency can bring about creative insight, spontaneous joy, and pride in the community of which we are a member. Decision-making and accountability become opportunities for a comforable belongingness and not oppressive burdens. Coping with self-sufficiency in community can be a disheartening enterprise or it can be a fascinating exercise in communal communication.

COMPETITION

Competition is an element that makes communal coping a very frustrating life-style. Competition should not be necessary in the religious or priestly life. Competition should not be necessary to enhance relationships nor should "apostolic jealousy" be fostered so that only the multi-talented feel at home. We can often observe that some community behavior fosters that rivalry created between two people in order to enhance the relationships of one of them with a third party, usually a superior authority figure. This kind of rivalry leads to childish dependency and not to the kind of normal effective reliance on each member that enhances community life.

When one feels self-sufficient and has resolved childish dependency needs, then there is no need to idealize those in authority and there is no need to be suspicious of normal friendship. True self-sufficiency leans toward normal dependency upon the community. Self-sufficiency should not be confused with a feeling of omnipotence. Many today, are wrestling with feelings of omnipotence; they are not really self-sufficient but establishing fears and distance so as to maintain their own masks of non-involvement in communal goals, dreams, and apostolate. Knowing I am part of a community but still self-sufficient does not mean that I spread myself so thin that I can control all variables or assume that I have more power than I really have. I am not always in competition. Self-sufficiency puts competition in the proper perspective and allows me to relate to the other community members in a way which is most meaningful and compelling.

LONELINESS

The last psychological factor in coping with community which we will briefly reflect upon today is loneliness. Effective coping in community will mean that I must learn to accept a certain sense of loneliness even though I may live with several other persons. "You mean aloneness," might be your first reaction. Not primarily. I mean the gut level feeling that I am all alone. As a clinician I wish to remind you that loneliness is a feeling all people experience at various times in life; it is not the priority of ecclesial communities. Loneliness is an acute feeling of twentieth century mankind amidst his technology and age of machine. Loneliness is a demonstration to me of original sin which has left us emotionally imperfect.

Loneliness need not be just a painful experience. Once we acknowledge the rough edges of this feeling, we can learn to develop a creative use of loneliness which leads not to depression but to creativity. Loneliness is an experience of being apart from the group and we are then most keenly aware of our individuality. It is out of this experience of separation and the consequent experience of reunion that further individualization and healing occurs.

Creatively, we can develop a sense of unlonely aloneness. We can enjoy spending time with ourselves and by ourselves doing things we enjoy. We must have time alone to commune with God, in order to know the nature of relationship with others, and in order to understand commitment to the community and to one's self. A coherent and sustaining way of life is gained not only from one's community but also from the sense of faith which emerges in clarity from the experience of loneliness and from the need for increased communication and sharing which is the healthy result that an experience of loneliness can bring. Loneliness allows for a creative opportunity to adequately manage leisure time. "To kill time" is another horrible cliché. Leisure allows us to affirm the being of all that is by not striving to do anything. Loneliness can make leisure the alleluia experience it is meant to be.

SUMMARY

Coping with community means a lot of agenda when we view it from its psychotheological perspective. We have touched upon a few of these factors in coping: affirmation, health, healing, responsibility, anger, competition, self-sufficiency, limits, loneliness. Effective coping with community requires both awareness of the stability of the community and the transition taking place in community. Stability and transition are interconnected elements which allow for progress: both must be present; neither sacrificed. Coping with community must be an evolving achievement. Coping, properly realized, will make community living a value to which we are intimately associated and in which we confidently believe.

Richard J. Gilmartin is a full-time psychotherapist at the House of Affirmation. In addition, he is an associate professor in the department of counselor education at Worcester State College, Massachusetts. Previously he was Psychological Counselor at Worcester State College, Director of Counseling and instructor in the Graduate School at Assumption College, Massachusetts, Chairman of the Psychology Department at St. Francis College, and Supervising Psychologist at the Religious Consultation Center of the Diocese of Brooklyn, New York. His undergraduate education was at St. Francis College, New York. His graduate education was at Fordham University, New York University, and St. John's University.

CHAPTER TWO

COPING WITH HUMANITY
Richard J. Gilmartin

DISSATISFACTION WITH SELF AND SELF-IMAGES
. . . OBSTACLES TO LIVING A FULL HUMAN LIFE
. . . SEXUALITY AND CELIBACY IN CREATIVE
FUSION

After listening to Father Kane's talk, I feel like discarding what I wanted to say, and just give my "Amen" to what he said. He said a lot of what I would like to say, and said it much better than I could have. He sets a standard for us that is difficult to attain.

Some time ago I was talking to a psychologist from Clark University who does his main therapeutic work in running groups. He told me that he has a constant fear that someday he is going to hold a group session and nobody is going to come. I, too, have an abiding fantasy that someday I am going to stand before an audience, open my mouth, and nothing is going to come out. I think I tell you that just to be sure something is coming out.

Father Kane said he had some misgivings about being a secular priest who was asked to speak on community. I share a similar feeling in being a married person speaking on celibacy. That, to me, seems somewhat incongruent too. It leaves me wondering what I am going to do.

I have to tell you about a bad habit of mine. On those nights that I do get home for dinner, much to my wife's chagrin I tend to fall asleep shortly after dinner, usually while sitting in the living room. This is especially true on Friday night and last night, being Friday, was no exception. I fell asleep around seven, my wife woke me — to go to bed — around eleven, and I was completely awake at four a.m. There is not much else to do at four in the morning except read, so I started reading an article by Timothy Leary.

Leary should be well-known to you Bostonians: native of Massachusetts, parochial school educated, student at Holy Cross, Harvard faculty member. He advocates a type of hedonistic philosophy, a kind of hedonistic approach to life, with which most of us would disagree. Yet he rekindled an idea in me. It is a concept of which we often lose sight. It is that we really do not know what constitutes "mental health." We talk a lot about it, but what really constitutes the mentally healthy person? Leary has a conception of what the mentally healthy person should be that is alien to what I might feel, and probably what you might feel. Yet, what does it really mean to be "mentally healthy"?

The use of the word "feeling" tends to identify me. "Feeling" has become kind of a cultic word that is associated with those who are into sensitivity groups and that kind of awareness thing. I am not sure that there is where I am really at, although I do have a great deal of sympathy for that approach.

The second feeling I had this morning was again wondering why I am coming here today and what I represent within this particular group. Today is a very significant day to me. It is the Feast of St. Francis. Five years ago, I left the Franciscans. I left religious life as a teaching brother for a number of reasons that are too many to go into now, but not without a great deal of pain and a great deal of separation anxiety. So great was this that for a long time, in fact sometimes even now, I have dreams about being back functioning as a religious, functioning as a Franciscan. Leaving religious life, although difficult, was relatively easy; escaping from it is much more difficult.

I came out, took a job teaching at a secular college, was

happy, led the life of a bachelor for approximately three years, and then met a very wonderful woman whom I love very much, and whose love for me I feel very strongly, and got married. I find myself happy with my life and thank God that I have a good marriage.

Yet I still feel the pull, the tug, of religious life. Your way of life has gotten into my very spirit and being, my blood, my thinking. It is very much a part of me. So I am talking to you today looking back from my experiences as a celibate religious and also from the perspective of a married man. It is as one who made a celibate commitment, and who changed that commitment to a different direction, and is now trying to think about it and evaluate it, that I speak to you today.

The topic that we are talking about today is "Coping With Humanity," but if you look down at the sub-title, you see it is "Dissatisfaction with self and self-images . . . obstacles to living a full human life . . . sexuality and celibacy in creative fusion." From this I took it to mean that my topic was coping with sexuality so that it can somehow become a creative impetus for our lives.

I did much as Father Kane did when he saw that word "coping." I too looked it up to get a more precise definition of the word. I had used it once before. When I was at the State College in Massachusetts, we saw the impending budgetary crisis which was to result in a cutback in the amount of money the State was going to allocate for higher education. To prepare for this we felt that the first thing we had to do was to somehow be prepared to demonstrate accountability for what we were doing. So I was asked to serve on a task-force to develop a rationale for having counseling services within our college. Quite by accident I fell onto this same word "coping." I see the whole function of education as helping people to cope with life, i.e., to come to terms with life and to live it successfully. Education, at least traditionally, provides the intellectual tools for coping and I see counseling as attempting to provide the emotional tools. It helps people to deal with their emotions, their mental functions, their feelings, and to bring these into concert with their whole being so that they can more effectively cope with life.

There is another meaning to that word which has also been alluded to here today. "Cope" is really a military term. It comes from the French "couper" which means "to deliver a blow" to somebody. Its original meaning was coping with somebody in battle, engaging in a kind of adversary encounter. I think this is an aspect of the word that we do not mean here. Coping with our humanity should not mean fighting with it, nor engaging in a kind of adversary encounter with our humanness. Much of our present problem comes from approaching our psychophysiological selves as if they were something that had to be subdued or tamed. This is not true just of religious, or of the Church. It is something that is in many people's lives. Part of our problem is that we were taught to approach our humanity in some sort of adversary way as if it were a foe to be subdued. I am sure you were taught that the best way to preserve celibacy was to avoid interaction with the opposite sex. I do not think that is a realistic approach. Just as making obedience the main Christian virtue and centering our lives around this virtue as a way of subduing our so-called "baser selves" is not a realistic approach because it hinders our maturation; so, too, avoidance is not effective in dealing with celibacy.

I think this is not effective because our humanity, our human needs, will not thus be denied without extracting a terrible price in depression, loneliness, feelings of isolation, guilt, alienation, feelings of inadequacy, and a general discontent and unhappiness. What it does not lead to is a viable spirituality.

Religious life should offer the chance to achieve a spiritual richness, to reach a full expression of our personality, to fully express what it means to be human. Frustrating the human side of ourselves leads to none of this. Rather it leads to a deadening of our spiritual fervor. Oh, we may stick to the outward forms of religious expression, but real spirituality, the viable spiritual drive, is not there. We practice a dull, uninspired religion and our personalities too are dull, flat, and uninteresting.

Expressing our humanness is not an easy thing to do. Functioning with our being in concert, rather than dichotomized, is not an easy thing to do. But this difficulty is not unique to religious. Achieving a successful marriage is not an easy thing to do, either, because it means dealing with a lot of things inside ourselves. So, too, being effective, spiritually oriented human beings means dealing with what is inside ourselves. If we compare the statistics between the failure rate in marriage and religious life, we see a remarkable similarity. The divorce rate and the number leaving religious life after final commitment, about 25% and climbing, is the same.

The word "failure" is not a good one, because marriages can end without their being failures and religious can make changes in vocation decisions without their being failures. But if we look at these changes as individuals moving toward something they really desired, and then not being able to achieve this desire, and feeling it necessary to change their direction, we must ask the question "Why?" Why do religious fail, in this latter sense of the term? Why do not religious become the kind of people they want to be? Whether they leave or not, they can still be failures; they can fail and leave or fail and stay, but in both cases they are failures.

There are probably several reasons for this, and today I would like to take a look at just a few of these that I think are significant. One of these is that people enter religious life, or marriage, with certain expectations that are never met. A friend of mine, who to all, at least out-

ward, appearances has a good marriage and a healthy
family, said to me that if he had really known what marriage was going to be like he would never have gotten
married. I have heard religious say the same thing. Looking back over fifteen or thirty or forty-five years in religion, if they had known what religious life was going to
be like, they would never have entered. Now, because of
age, or insecurities, or whatever, they do not choose to
make a vocational change. This is sad. It is sad when married people say it. It is even sadder when religious say it.

I could not say that. If I knew how my life was going
to be before I entered religion, would I still have entered?
Yes, unqualifiedly yes. Although I have no long perspective
on which to judge marriage, would I still get married
knowing now what marriage is like? Yes. It is sad when
somebody says, "Gee, if I had known . . . No."

Secondly, it is possible that either married people or
religious are unaware of the demands that the life is going
to impose on them, and now they are either unable, or
unwilling, to meet these demands. This is a little different
than entering with expectations that will not be met.

I would like to focus on this, but before we do, let us
talk about the third possibility. This one is that personality factors interfere with, or render someone incapable of
living religious life or both giving to it and getting from
it what he should. This is a big possibility, and the same
thing operates in marriage too. Personality factors in one
or both partners interfere with relating in marriage in
the way and to the degree that the relationship demands.

What we are talking about is mental illness. I know
Father Kane said we should focus on mental health, and
I agree with that. But there is the other side of the coin
too, and that is the mental illness problem.

There has been a lot of research done on the question of
whether or not mental illness is more common among religious than lay people and the results are conflicting and

ambiguous. One early study done at the Seton Institute in Baltimore, I think back in the thirties or early forties, found that the incidence of severe mental illness among religious was much lower than in the general population. That kind of conclusion dominated thinking for awhile and some churchmen, in their not atypical triumphalistic approach, flaunted this as "proving" that religious life and celibacy was actually a healthier way of life.

But then someone took a harder look at the data on which those conclusions were based and said, "Hey, wait a minute." If we just do one thing, if we remove one group from the study, look what happens. If we remove from the study those people whose mental illness is directly traceable to venereal infection, i.e., to syphilis or gonorrhea, then the opposite results obtain. The incidence of mental illness becomes higher in the clergy and religious. Syphilis and gonorrhea are relatively low, understandably so, in religious people, while quite high in the general population and, left untreated, they can wreak havoc on mental functioning.

If I were to evaluate, on the basis of my experience from having worked with clergy, religious, and lay people, and from my interpretation of the literature, my impression is that there probably is no difference. Emotional problems in religious are probably neither more nor less common than they are in the laity.

One fact there is, however, and that is that religious life can act as a "trigger" for mental illness for certain kinds of personalities and, in this sense, can be seen as a causative agent. It can precipitate emotional problems in certain kinds of personalities. But so too can college life, so too can military life, so too can any kind of particular life style. But there is a certain kind of personality pattern that will get triggered by religious life.

I think, secondly, that problems tend to take different forms in religious than they do in the population as a whole. I was talking just recently to another therapist, and he was discussing a Sister that he had been seeing. He found the profile quite remarkable in that when she first came to him she was extremely withdrawn, minimally communicative, and manifested some other symptomatology which would be traditionally regarded as schizophrenic. But after about three sessions with him she just blossomed out. She was communicating coherently and fluidly, and was insightful into the kind of needs she had, and began developing strategies to meet these needs. She was suddenly more assertive and exhibited other healthier behavior. Of course he would have liked to attribute these changes to his own curative powers, but really knew better. The fact is that she was not schizophrenic, but her environment was contributing to her production of schizophrenic-like symptoms.

Some symptoms seen in religious are not as severe when seen in people outside, and frequently have a different meaning. Culture shapes symptom patterns and religious life presents a culture all its own.

There was a study done, I think it was last year, under a National Institute of Mental Health grant, on the Sudanese to determine the patterns of mental illness in that African culture. It came up with some interesting findings that are relevant to what we are talking about. The Sudanese have a high incidence of hysteria and hysterical-like symptoms. Today, these are relatively rare in our culture. Hysteria is traditionally more common in women than men. Just the word "hysteria" which comes from the Greek "hystos", meaning "womb", would indicate this. In Sudan, they found a lot of women with hysterical symptoms.

Depression, which is our number one mental health problem, is unknown in the Sudan. Not one incidence of it was found. Schizophrenia is found in both cultures, but the form it took was different. The Sudanese tended to have a high incidence of hebephrenic type schizophrenia, where impulsive bizarre behavior is the predominant symptom. This occurs in our culture too, but we tend to get more of the paranoid type of schizophrenia, where suspicion is the most marked symptom. Again, they had none of this. There was no incidence of paranoia or paranoid flavoring to schizophrenia in the Sudanese culture.

The point that we are trying to make is that culture shapes symptoms. There probably is a predisposition or propensity for the disturbance present, but our culture plays a large part in deciding the kind of symptoms that we are going to permit ourselves to have, and I mean that quite literally. We give ourselves permission to develop certain symptoms.

Religious do the same thing. You have a culture unto yourselves and the kinds of problems you have, although not unique to you, are shaped by that culture.

If I were to look at religious, from my experience, to learn what are their more common problems, I see two. I think religious are more heavily motivated from guilt than is the lay population. That is to say that, aware of it or not, guilt is a strong motivating force in what they do. I certainly do not mean all religious are motivated from guilt. We could probably even exclude everybody here today. But what I am saying is that the incidence of acting out unconscious feelings of guilt is higher than you would find in the population as a whole.

Secondly, I find that religious have more difficulties in the area of interpersonal relationships. This is even more common than the guilt we just spoke about. This is a problem in achieving and sustaining deep intimate relationships with others. We will say more about this.

About ten years ago a prominent psychiatrist, who also happens to be a Catholic and has a practice largely composed of clergy and religious, was quoted as saying something to the effect that to be successful in leading religious life you had to be either very sick or very healthy; the person in the middle is the one who has problems with it. I am not sure I would agree with that today, but there is a message in there.

We spoke before about some of the things that attract people to religious life. One of the major insights given to us by Sigmund Freud is that all behavior is multi-motivated. In any significant decision that we have to make, and the decision to enter religious life is certainly a significant decision, there is more than one factor that impels us toward the decision that we finally reach. Some of these factors, or reasons, are conscious and some are unconscious; some of them are healthy and some of them are unhealthy. This is the human condition and we cannot do much about it. The best we can hope for is that more of our reasons for doing a thing are healthy and conscious. The unconscious ones are going to be there; the unhealthy ones are also going to be there. But we hope that the major portion of our motivating pattern is healthy.

Too often for those attracted to religious life, as is true in many other professions or ways of life, the major portion of their motivating pattern is not conscious and healthy, but rather unconscious and unhealthy. Religious life does provide a certain kind of environment, at least it did in the past. It provided a protective kind of cocoon and for the person who felt inadequate to the task of coping with the outside world, this protection was fine. Religious life also provided a protective cocoon for the person who had trouble relating to others in a deep, meaningful way. Because of its single sex environment it does not place the same kind of demands on the person that, for example, marriage places.

If I am going to relate to someone else in a way that is mutually satisfying, I am going to have to deal with an awful lot of things inside myself. I have to deal with my sexuality, or possibly my homosexuality. I have to deal with my anger, and we all get angry, as Father Kane mentioned. I have to deal with my anger both in being able to express it and, reflectively, with other peoples' becoming angry at me. If I do not deal with my own anger, I have problems, and I have to be able to deal with others' anger without being shattered, broken, or coming apart from it. Religious life offered at least the appearances for being protected from that.

Now as the life changes and we, as a people, are becoming much more aware of peoples' human needs for intimacy and closeness, the protective cocoon is unravelling. Religious are looking for the fulfillment of their personal human needs, and rightly so. But some of the older religious, and by this I do not mean older in years but rather older in their patterns of adaptation, who hid behind this protective cocoon and, in fact, were seen as the ideal religious because they were self-sufficient and work-committed, are now having trouble. Religious life gave support to a neurotic pattern of adjustment and those who adjusted to it were seen as productive members. But now, as the life opens up, and others are demanding greater personal fulfillment, they are having trouble dealing with this; they are having trouble dealing with the interpersonal relatedness that is demanded, and all that this entails.

Besides dealing with my sexuality and anger, interpersonal relating also demands that I expose myself, that I take the risk in letting you see me as I am. Even in my being here today, I could be a very heady person and stand here and give you all types of intellectual reactions to our topic. But you would sit there and listen, and then in a half-hour forget it. What you will remember from me today is any bit of myself, any bit of my personalism, that I can share with you. But doing this is a risky thing. I can be rejected, ridiculed, hurt by you in any one of a hundred ways. But I have to take that risk.

I felt a risk in telling you about my background, because

you could have reacted negatively towards me for that. You could have regarded me as something like a Benedict Arnold, or worse. Yet I felt that if I was really going to say what was in my mind and heart, I had to expose myself to you. I could have given a very academic lecture here today on successful and unsuccessful adjustments, but for the most part we would have been wasting each other's time. I think the same is true in relating to each other on an individual basis.

When I left religious life I got one very good piece of advice. It was from a layman, who was also a psychologist and a good friend. He said, "Be sure to re-live your adolescence." I was in mid-thirties, knew a fair amount of psychology, and felt I had long since moved past adolescence, and did not really take that statement too seriously. But what he was saying was important. I had to go out and experience several relationships and to experience myself in different relationships, thereby working out some things in my personality, before I was ready to make a commitment again. I had to do much of what the adolescent should do as he moves toward an adult commitment to one human being. If I had attempted marriage when I first left, it would have been disastrous. I needed to experience intimacy at different levels, and to deal with my reactions to it, before I was ready to make a permanent intimate commitment.

Analogously, the same is true of you. Before you can live the ideal of celibacy, you must first come to grips with an awful lot of stuff. We are not just talking about unhealthy stuff either. You must work through adolescent sexuality before you can be fulfilled in a celibate commitment. Let us talk about some of the things that must be done.

Before this let us get one thing out of the way. If you try to be celibate by denying sexuality, by running away from it, by treating it as if it did not exist, by treating yourself as if you were two distinct beings one of which is physical and the other spiritual and which are at war with each other and your only hope is that eventually the spiritual is going to triumph, you are in trouble. You are apt to feel depressed, lonely, isolated, and you are not going to be fulfilled as a human being.

Be leery of the kind of spiritual advice you permit yourself to take. There are many good spiritual writers, but there are also a good many whose spiritual writings are more reflective of their personal emotional problems than of ways to God. For example, that story that was told of St. Aloysius Gonzaga that he never looked his mother in the face lest he be tempted, probably, if true, said more about St. Aloysius' oedipal conflict than it did about his spirituality or his sanctity.

Another thing that will happen if you try to deal with sexuality through a rigid repressive control is that the sexuality will break through. It will break through in a variety of symptoms. It could come out in sexual preoccupation, so that sexual imagery becomes an obsession that cannot be avoided. It could come out as homosexual ideas, or masturbatory habits. The former does not necessarily mean that one is a homosexual, but rather both could be symptomatic of attempting to deal with sexuality in a repressive way. This is especially true when the thoughts are obsessional in nature, or the actions are compulsive. They are both symptoms.

What can we do about our sexuality? Let us say that we are not using celibacy as a way of avoiding intimacy, or a way of avoiding facing our sexual or emotional frigidity. But rather celibacy has other meanings for us, meanings in terms of non-commitment to one person: to be free to commit ourselves to ideals, or to many people. What can we do about our own sexuality?

First of all, we need to recognize that we are sexual beings. This is number one. Sexuality is part of our humanness. I am sure that we all give intellectual assent to this idea, but we must also feel it in our hearts. We have to really feel ourselves to be persons with sexuality. Just because you gave up the direct expression of your sexuality does not mean that you are not going to feel its urgings; it does not mean that you are not going to have sexual fantasies. You have to become comfortable with this as part of your human reality.

Something happened to me that brought this home very sharply. I do not mean to be too anecdotal because that tends to set me up as the ideal, and in no way do I feel that way. It is just that I am talking to you from some of my own personal struggles with these issues.

I did my internship as a psychologist in a public, hospital-affiliated clinic. I was a religious and, for the first time, I was having to deal with women therapeutically. My supervisor was a non-Catholic. I would diligently prepare my cases, laying out very eruditely for his scrutiny what I saw to be the dynamics of a personality. I was really taken aback when his only comment would be something like, "How were her legs?" or "Was she sexy?" At first I could not answer these questions and they embarrassed me. But my embarrassment was saying that I was not dealing with my feelings. What he was saying to me was that I had to be aware of my own humanity, my maleness, my personness, because I had to respond to her on this level. That does not mean that we would become sexually involved, but I had to be aware that she was a woman and that I was a man. That was reality. I had to first recognize and then be comfortable with my own personhood, and sexuality is part of this.

This is part of your relationships too. You must be aware of, and sensitive to, that. This is the first thing; accept the fact that I am a sexual human being and, hand-in-hand with this, be comfortable with this acceptance.

The second thing is that I must recognize that sexuality

is neither overwhelming nor uncontrollable. Some of those who have written about sexual morality would give us this impression. They imply that sex is a passion that lies buried inside of us and if we allow the slightest expression of it, we will be overwhelmed by it. As taking the finger out of the dike will permit all the water to gush forth, so too liberated sexuality will inundate us.

This kind of reaction is not true just of sexuality; there is a tendency to approach many of our emotions the same way. Also, it is not true just of religious, but is common throughout our culture. Perhaps one of the reasons why the movie "Jaws" is so popular is that what the audience is doing is playing with their own unconscious, with their own "primitive things" coming up from "the deep" and wreaking havoc. After they have played with this danger they find themselves nice and safe in their theatre seat. That is, at least partly, what makes this movie so enticing for so many people.

I have to come to recognize that sexuality is not an uncontrollable thing; that if I give in to it, I will not be overwhelmed. If there is a problem with control, it is more likely indicative of a totally different conflict rather than a problem with sex per se. It is similar to the problem of a person who is a compulsive eater, who has to ingest food continuously even to the detriment of his health. His problem is not overwhelming hunger, nor is it the fact that he once tasted food and now has an uncontrollable urge. No, it is a symptom of something else. There is a deeper, underlying conflict that has surfaced in this one small area. The same is true of problems in sexual control.

Marriage is no panacea for sexual problems. If I look at the two states, I would say that sex is no easier, nor more difficult, to control in marriage than in religious life. It is obvious that in both states of life some control is necessary. Just because someone is married and has a wife who provides a sexual relationship does not mean that oth-

er women are not attractive. I am sure the same is true
for women finding other men than their husbands to be
attractive. Even though there is a good marital relationship and the involvement with each other is deep, I can
still find other people attractive. What the good marital
relationship and deep involvement means is that I would
not get sexually involved with someone else. First of all,
because I know how much it would hurt my wife, and
secondly, because I have made a commitment to her to
work at a relationship exclusively with her. That is the
reason why I stay faithful to her. But that does not mean
that I do not feel urgings, have fantasies or ideas. That
is part of humanness, but it is not uncontrollable.

If I am going to accept my sexuality, and be comfortable with it, I also have to recognize that it is not an
uncontrollable thing.

The third thing that I think is important is to be careful where you draw your defensive perimeters. Be careful
where you begin controlling the expression of sexuality.
It is obvious that, if you take your celibate commitment
seriously and see it as precluding a direct expression of
sexuality, then some control is necessary.

Some people make the distinction between sexual needs
and genital needs and say that we have to satisfy sexual
needs and need not satisfy genital needs. That is probably
true and if that distinction helps you, fine. I would rather
approach it from the perspective of being careful where
you draw your defensive perimeter.

In attempting to control the direct expression of sexuality, we have tended too often to go too far back and denied
ourselves other needs. The need for affection, for intimacy,
for understanding, for sharing myself with others, too
frequently were sacrificed in the attempt to control sexuality. But these very real needs cannot be sacrificed without a warping of our personality. If I do not satisfy these
needs I open myself for other problems, only one of which

is depression. In trying to control my sexual expression, I must be careful to still find ways to satisfy my affectionate needs, my needs for closeness with others, my needs for sharing myself, my ideas, my feelings with others, and my needs for getting understanding back from others.

Pope Paul VI made the statement that the best safeguard for chastity is community. I suspect that he was implying something of what we are talking about now. There must be a place where I can get affection and love and intimacy and warmth. Community has to be something more than hotels with a chapel. Community has to be something more than a place where the members only talk to each other over alcohol. It has to be more than that.

I am sure this has been said hundreds of times and the literature is replete with references on the need to create real community. But in many cases real community is not being created and religious are suffering.

This is not to say that a religious house is a place where there is one long sensitivity session either. That would be unreal and, although sensitivity sessions can have a certain value for certain people, we could not sustain that type of intimacy for any length of time. There is also a danger in having people know all the right words for relating. I am sure you have encountered the kind of person, confrere or Sister, who says such things as "Thank you for sharing," or "I can really feel what you're feeling," and so on, but without there being any depth to their verbal attempts at intimacy. They know all the "right formulas" for relating, but do not really relate. They have substituted one externalized form of behavior for another. That is not community either.

Community is a place where I can share in the affection and intimacy of a group. It is a place where I can go and know that they care about me and that I care about them.

I work about an hour's drive from where I live, and I leave the house at eight in the morning and, quite frequently, am not back home until ten at night. But when I start home after a day's work, I feel a lot of warmth. I really want to get home, to get to where there is someone that I really love and who really loves me. If I had found that in a religious community, I would not have left. I did not, but I believe it is possible.

A real community is where I can be affirmed for who I am, not for what I do. Not because I am good over at the school, or am an effective pastor, or a good cook, am I valued, but just because I am. If I am receiving this acceptance I can move out and accept other people the same way.

To achieve this, religious communities may have to stop being organized around work-oriented groups, and start being organized around person-oriented groups. It is a reality that some persons may not be able to get along with other persons and they should not be in the same group. There may have to be some choice as to with whom we are going to live. No one told me whom to marry, with whom to spend my life. Nobody denied me those choices. Why should it be denied to you? Religious communities should be person-oriented communities, and you should not live with a certain group just because you happen to work at a certain place. Real community is a difficult thing to establish and has to be worked at; we should have some choice as to with whom we are going to work to establish it. But if we do not have real community, our problems are going to multiply and people are going to continue to suffer.

Let me close by saying a few words about responsibility. Father Kane saw responsibility as the basis for community. I would like to take it a step further. Realizing I have no special expertise in theology, and speaking solely of what it means to me to be a Christian, I see responsibility as the basis for Christian morality. This responsibility goes two ways. First of all, it goes to me. I must be responsible for myself.

If I could remove one word from the list of vices, I would take out "selfishness." Selfishness is not a vice, it is a virtue. You should be selfish. When people go through psychotherapy they usually leave with, if nothing else, the conviction that "I am the most important person in my life." That is basic. I have to fulfill my needs as a human being, I have to fulfill myself as a person, I have to be the most important person in my life.

I really get tired of hearing self-sacrificing people, who are usually very boring to start with, say that they are living their lives for their wife, or their children, or their Church, or their religious order, or their God. I do not think it is real. I think they are cloaking their self-seeking, hiding it from themselves, denying it, and then becoming resentful and bitter when other people do not adulate and reward them for their self-sacrificingness. We have to acknowledge our selfishness and permit ourselves to be number one.

Where we Christians differ is that selfishness does not stop with ourselves. I have to want for others the same things I want for myself. I have to want for other people to fulfill their potential too. Even more than wanting it for them, I have to work for that. The yardstick of Christian morality is love of neighbor as you love yourself. The equative word there is "as": not more than, nor less than, nor instead of, but rather as much as. I have to reach out to other people and help them find the same things in life that I desire for myself.

I see this message in the Eucharist. Besides being a sacrament, the Eucharist is also an exemplar. As Christ made himself nourishment for us, we must make ourselves nourishment for other people.

That is also what should be exemplified in community. If it is, it will flow over into your particular pastoral work and people will respond to your richness as a human being.

Sister Philomena Agudo is a member of the Franciscan Missionaries of Mary. She is originally from the Philippines, and it was there that she earned her B.A. from Our Lady of Loretto College, and her M.A. from Ateneo University. She was a missionary in Indonesia and Singapore where she engaged in counseling work with religious and lay persons. She received her doctorate in Pastoral Psychology and Counseling from Boston University. Before joining the staff of the House of Affirmation, she worked at Boston's South End Center for Alcoholism, at Lemuel Shattuck Hospital with terminal cancer patients, and at the Danielsen Counseling Center, Boston University. She is the author of "Contributions of Wilfred Daim and Viktor Frankl to Counseling in the Context of a Religious Community of Women."

CHAPTER THREE

COPING WITH MEANING
Philomena Agudo

If there is anyone well equipped with the universal and personal meanings of human existence, it is the religious professional. Yet it must be admitted that the mere possession of meanings is not adequate to enable a person to function as a stable and happy religious or minister. One needs to cope with these meanings in order to make life fruitful and rewarding. I refer to "existential meaning" according to Viktor Frankl:

> The term "existential" may be used in three ways: to refer to (1) existence itself, i.e., the specifically human mode of being; (2) the meaning of existence; and (3) the striving to find a concrete meaning in personal existence, that is to say, the will to meaning.[1]

The spiritual dimension of humanity spurs people to seek the meaning of their existence. There is in every human being that desire for happiness; but when a person pursues happiness directly for itself, it eventually eludes him. Happiness is the by-product or the after-effect of achieving a meaningful life.

For Frankl, personal meaning is most important. He considers values as personal meanings that eventually become universal. However, if we analyze existential meaning, we come face to face with both the universal purpose of human existence (which is the consequence of one's religion and philosophy of life), and the personal meaning a particular individual derives from it. Although Freud considers religion a contributing factor in neurosis, Frankl believes that it provides a person with a spiritual anchor, giving him/her a sense of security which he/she can find nowhere else. Religion is indestructible. Even psychosis cannot destroy it. Aside from universal meaning, every individual needs a personal meaning for his or her life. This meaning is derived from values, and is discovered in love, joy, and even suffering.

Frankl further points to the fact that a meaningless life results in a certain kind of neurosis — "noogenic", in which the individual suffers from the aimlessness, the emptiness of life. This condition implies a spiritual problem, a moral conflict, or an existential vacuum; and, according to him, one cannot clearly distinguish between spiritual distress and mental disease.[2]

While Freud finds the root of distressing disorders in the anxiety caused by conflicting and unconscious motives, Frankl traces it to the failure of the sufferer to find meaning and a sense of responsibility in his or her existence.

THE MEANING OF LIFE

With regard to a universal meaning to life itself, there is no problem for the religious who puts his or her faith in Divine Providence. The ultimate meaning of life is well defined. It is clear that belief in a metaphysical concept of God as part of a system of firmly held convictions is of psychotherapeutic importance. It becomes for the individual an unfailing source of emotional security. Such faith immeasurably strengthens the human ability to cope with vicissitude, and thus insures a meaningful life.

Pointing to personal meaning in one's life, Frankl stresses the fact that:

> One should not search for an abstract meaning of life. Everyone has his own specific vocation or mission in life; everyone must carry out a concrete assignment that demands fulfillment. Therein he cannot be replaced, nor can his life be repeated. Thus, everyone's task is as unique as is his specific opportunity to implement it.[3]

THE MEANING OF DEATH

The meaning of death, just as the meaning of life, is

known to every religious professional. Although there is the pain of loss, death is not wholly tragic. Its meaning has elements of joy and hope. Finality or temporality is an essential characteristic of human life, and thus is one of the factors in its meaningfulness. Death as a temporally ultimate boundary does not cancel the meaning of life, but rather is the very factor that constitutes its meaning. This outer limit enables the inner limits to add to the meaning of human life. The uniqueness of every human person makes him or her irreplaceable. Just as the faith of the religious person provides meaning to life, this same faith also provides meaning to human finiteness, experienced as death.

PERSONAL MEANING

Personal meaning is relative in that it is possessed by a particular person involved in a specific situation. A person's spiritual attitude includes the physical as well as the psychic components of human nature. A spiritual attitude derives from and reflects the values that the individual possesses. Hence, as individual perspectives vary, so do values. Frankl classifies values as "creative," "experiential," and "attitudinal."

> Life can be made meaningful by what we give to the world in terms of our creation or productivity; by what we take from the world in terms of our own experience; and by the attitude we choose toward events that happen in our life.[4]

Life without values is meaningless, and inevitably results in some kind of pathology. Yet life can remain basically meaningful even when it is neither fruitful in creation nor rich in experience for the individual. It can be so, because meaning derives from the person's attitude toward the factors that limit life. The opportunity to realize attitudinal values is present even when a person is confronted by events beyond his/her control, and toward which he/she can act only by acceptance.

TENSION FROM MEANING

There is tension between universal and personal meanings. This tension is experienced by every human being. It is due to the fact that universal meanings are the ideals — what life ought to be. For the religious person, the universal meaning of life is the attainment of holiness in a particular style of life. Personal meanings, on the other hand, relate to what life actually is. In order to assimilate our own personal meaning into the universal meaning of holiness, we must take into account our weaknesses and limitations as well as our potentialities within the stresses and burdens of life. Hence we experience tension. In coping with tension we need to use our freedom and our sense of responsibility.

I do not intend to deal with universal meanings in detail. We are all aware of them, and we all have them. Personal meaning is my concern right now. This is where each individual differs from the other. This is where stress and conflict begins. I would like to include at this point a diagram to illustrate what I have been saying.

COPING WITH MEANING

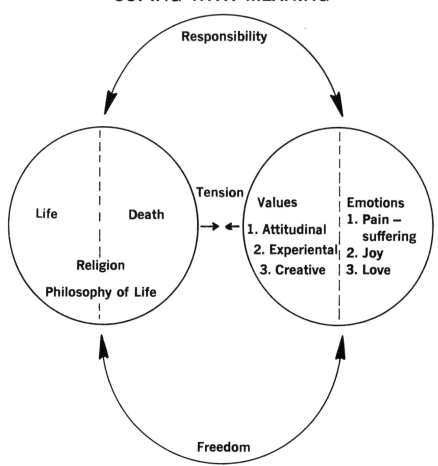

Frankl considers people as possessing three dimensions: the somatic, the psychic, and the spiritual.[5] There is an intertwining of these three dimensions such that each affects the other. It is therefore possible that one who is in spiritual distress could also be afflicted by mental illness. A person who is mentally or emotionally disturbed needs help physically and emotionally, as well as spiritually. The spiritual life of the person cannot be ignored. Among the three dimensions, it is the spiritual dimension that moves the individual to find meaning in life.

It is surprising but also true that in spite of the universal meanings available to religious persons, they often lead meaningless lives. A particular person, for example, may be fully aware of the universal meaning of his or her existence but has not discovered a particular meaning for his or her own life. On the other hand, a religious person may have discovered a personal meaning, but there is tension between the universal meaning and the personal meaning. The religious can find himself/herself unable to harmonize these meanings.

VALUES

Before going into the harmonization of meanings, I would like to discuss the importance of values. Values are so important that without them, one cannot possibly discover a meaning to life. However, it is not sufficient merely to possess values. These values must flow from self-acceptance. No one can ever develop creative values unless he/she has accepted the fact that he/she is *someone*, and that there is the potential to be productive in one's life. How can one develop experiential values unless one realizes the capacity to experience the beautiful, the pleasant and the unpleasant, joy and sorrow, loving and being loved? To develop attitudinal values the person needs to accept his or her capacity to form attitudes with regard to events that happen in life. Values cannot exist when the individual does not accept his or her individuality which includes assets and liabilities, potentials and limitations.

With experiential values, the individual needs to appreciate those qualities and gifts which make possible the varied experiences in life. It is only after first appreciating oneself that a person develops the capacity to appreciate experiences. For example, one could never appreciate the value of a warm and true friendship unless one is convinced of his or her worthiness of such a relationship. Only then will the person be able to perceive the value of such an experience.

LOVE

From what we have already said, it is evident that attitudes play a very important role in making life meaningful. One can never appreciate the real value of love, joy and even suffering unless one has the right attitude. Let us now discuss love. The aspect of love that I would like to focus on is the main core of loving. Love is not simply an emotion nor does it end as an emotion. Rather, love is mainly a spiritual act. It is this spirituality which gives love its permanence. When you love, you actually love the spiritual core of the person. It is true that the physical aspect of the person is important, and love is expressed physically; but the physical expression is not the essence of love. Loving relationships happen only because there is a spiritual core in each person. Loving becomes meaningful only when the attitudinal value is its foundation. Love based on the attitude of pleasure alone is not love but a means of satisfying a need. Unless one possesses a personal spiritual value, and recognizes the spiritual value of the other person, there is no real love. Again, one is simply satisfying a human need. It is the spiritual dimension in humans that makes possible the loving relationship. Frankl presents love as spiritual. The physical expression is the after-effect, but the relationship rests in the spirit.

> Love is not deserved, it is unmerited — it is simply grace.
> . . . .
> Love enormously increases receptivity to the fullness of values. . . . For it is well known that love does not make one blind but seeing — able to see values.[6]

The most important aspect of love is its spiritual value.

It is only due to this spiritual value that commitment and permanency in love is possible. Since love occurs in the spiritual core that forms the lover and the beloved, he or she is therefore irreplaceable.

JOY

Joy is an intentional emotion. It is only when emotion exists in a relationship to values that the person can experience true joy. One can thus only experience joy when a definite meaning in personal life has been discovered by the individual. A feeling of elation without meaning is simply pleasure. Pleasure and joy are not the same. Joy can be experienced even in the midst of pain or suffering because joy is dependent on attitudes. We have all met persons who claim to have never experienced joy, or may have experienced joy as children, but somehow this joy has eluded them as adults. This malaise is often due to the pursuit of pleasure for its own sake, called the "pleasure principle." When pleasure is pursued for itself, joy eludes the person. True joy is the after-effect of a meaningful life. It is experienced when behavior is based on, and experiences are integrated into, a system of values. Thus one finds joy in friendship, in reading, in prayer, in being alone or in being with others. The circumstances which bring joy can vary from person to person. What is constant is the need for values to be realized. If one values human communication, then communication with others will be one of the sources of joy. But above all, a person who has never learned to accept himself/herself cannot experience true joy. A person who has degraded himself/herself in his/her own eyes can never be joyful. To the degree that there is self-acceptance, joy can be experienced.

SUFFERING

Suffering is a reality in life which many persons would rather avoid than accept. Suffering shapes and forms the life of every individual. It is one of the experiences that give meaning to life. Frankl points to the fact that human life can be fulfilled not only in creating and enjoying, but also in suffering.[7] Suffering can be a means of growth. Every time we go through a crisis in life, we suffer. The same crisis can be the occasion for two quite different results depending on how we handle it. We can allow the suffering to cripple or destroy us, or we can use it as a stepping stone to growth and maturity. Suffering actualizes attitudinal values. On the biological plane, pain acts as a warning system. On the psycho-spiritual level, suffering prevents apathy, thus providing chances for emotional growth and spiritual wisdom. If suffering is considered something to be avoided at any cost, it follows that the person is placing undue reliance on the "pleasure principle." Suffering is not to be sought after, nor tolerated when it can be remedied. However, it has to be accepted with the right attitude when it is beyond human means to remedy. The only constructive way of dealing with suffering is to accept it. Frankl mentions the effect of suffering when accepted with the right attitude: "In fact, we mature in suffering, grow because of it — it makes us richer and stronger."[8]

THE HARMONIZATION OF UNIVERSAL AND PERSONAL MEANINGS

How does one cope with the tensions brought about by "meaning"? Two important factors are necessary for successfully harmonizing universal and personal meanings: responsibility and freedom. Responsibility and freedom exist within the spiritual domain of every human being. Each individual is free, and freedom means that one is responsible for the realization of the meaning of his or her life. The reality of the transitoriness of life is an incentive to the individual to be responsible for the kind of life he/she wants to lead. Avoidance of responsibility produces neurotic fatalism.

We are responsible to others, to ourselves, to our consciences, and to that extra-human authority — God. We are responsible for our behavior, for the love we develop, and the joy we experience. We are also responsible for developing the means by which we cope with suffering. When depressed persons say, "I am depressed. I cannot do anything about it", they are betraying their attitude of irresponsibility. Therapy cannot achieve its goal unless the client is determined to be responsible. Through acceptance of responsibility we are able to harmonize what we actually are, our personal meaning in life, with the universal meaning we have as our goal — holiness. We must be careful not to reject our humanity as we are developing our personal meaning. We need to value and cherish our humanity, including our human weaknesses, in order to have a sufficiently strong base from which to take the kind of initiative that will result in strengthening ourselves and allowing the maturing process to happen in us. True responsibility has to emerge from the person. It is when we are responsible that we appreciate ourselves as persons. In fact, to be a person means to be responsible. Thus, a person is not an object to be manipulated by others, nor is he determined by environment and heredity. No situation in life, however negative, can take away the fact that we are responsible for the shaping of our lives. A thought occurs to me that I would like to share here. It is quite simply this: when God gave us the grace to consecrate our lives to Him, He had no intention at all of depriving us of our common sense. If we are to be responsible, we need to use our common sense. Let us not underestimate this precious gift of common sense which we need in order to remain sane and emotionally stable.

FREEDOM

In addition to responsibility, another tool for coping with meaning is freedom. Freedom implies the ability to handle one's instincts, one's biological inheritance, and one's personal environment. Freedom does not spring from the body or the psyche, but from the spirit. Humans are confined within the dimension of the body, and are driven by many forces from the psyche, but are free in the realm of the spirit. It is in this spiritual dimension that free choices are made. Frankl differentiates the neurotic from the healthy person by the use of freedom. The neurotic misunderstands his/her existence as: "this is the way I have to be," whereas the healthy person has the attitute: "I can always change."

An individual is free to make the choice between taking a purely fatalistic attitude toward his or her past, or learning something from it. A person may be bound by natural endowment or by environment, but he or she is free to develop an attitude and make decisions regarding these conditions. It is this freedom to decide what stance to take toward the conditions of one's life that gives proof of his/her humanity. Conditions do not determine the person, but the person determines whether he or she will cope with these conditions effectively.

Every human being is self-determining. This means that one can determine not only the course of one's life, but also can take a hand in shaping one's own character. Persons, therefore, are not only responsible for what they are, but are also responsible for becoming according to how they choose to behave. Instead of being crippled by conditions, humans construct themselves through the use of their freedom. No human person remains static; he or she continually decides what he or she will be in the next moment. The choices of every moment forge the person's character. Because of this freedom and the capacity to change, one can never predict with accuracy the future of a human being.

Clients sometimes say to me that there is no hope for them. They add that they were born into their present condition. Sometimes they blame the community they live in for their lack of hope. My response to them is that they do not have hope because they have decided not to hope, that they are using their freedom to crush hope in their lives. Just as we have the freedom to hope, we have the freedom to shape our character, our personality, despite limitations and negative influences.

I have always had a great admiration for Helen Keller. She proved to the world the freedom of the human spirit. Despite her physical limitations and handicaps, she proved that it is possible to attain an integrated and lovable personality. Her life of freedom gives all of us hope to overcome the negative forces which could hinder us from being whole and integrated. Because we, too, are free in the same way, we have no right to blame someone else for our failures and disappointments. Our freedom obliges us to accept total responsibility for the quality of life we lead.

Freedom and responsibility go hand in hand. One cannot be responsible unless one is free to make decisions. Likewise one cannot make good decisions unless one has a sense of responsibility toward oneself and others. Thus freedom can be misused. Because one is free to take a stand, many circumstances must be weighed. The pros and cons of decisions to be made must be considered. One has also to consider the consequences of a decision with questions like: Will it be beneficial or destructive to oneself or to others? Will this decision bring about growth and maturity, or will it lead to regression? Some people find it difficult to decide on anything. Indecisiveness seems to be the mark of their personalities. People who are indecisive are usually avoiding responsibility for their actions. This state robs them of joy, for one must be responsible to experience true joy.

To conclude, I would like to stress once again that one of the main features of human existence is the capacity to emerge from and rise above adversity, that is, to experience happiness even in the midst of negative conditions. Every human being is self-transcendent and self-determining. Due to these spiritual qualities, every individual, if he or she chooses, is able to reconcile and integrate, in short, to cope with the universal meaning of his or her existence, and the personal meanings discovered in particular situations in life, despite the tensions they occasionally bring.

REFERENCES

1. Viktor Frankl, *Man's Search for Meaning*, (New York: Simon and Schuster Inc., 1973), p. 159.
2. Viktor Frankl, *The Will to Meaning*, (New York: The World Publishing Co., 1969), p. 88.
3. Viktor Frankl, *Man's Search for Meaning*, p. 172.
4. Viktor Frankl, *The Doctor and the Soul*, (New York: Vintage Books, 1973), pp. 43-44.
5. Viktor Frankl, *The Doctor and the Soul*, p. x.
6. Ibid., p. 133.
7. Ibid., p. 106.
8. Ibid., p. 109.

Reverend Bernard J. Bush, S.J., is a member of the California Province of the Society of Jesus. He studied theology at Regis College, Willowdale, Ontario, and was ordained in 1965. He served as student chaplain at the University of San Francisco before assuming the post of spiritual director at the Jesuit theologate in Berkeley, California. From there he went to Boston State Hospital where he interned in Pastoral Psychology. In 1974, he joined the staff of the House of Affirmation and opened the satellite office in Boston. Father Bush has written numerous articles in the areas of spirituality and social justice, most notably in "The Way." He has been active in the directed retreat movement and has lectured on Ignatian spirituality, religious life, mental health, and social justice. The workshop on coping presented in this volume was sponsored by the Boston Office of the House of Affirmation.

CHAPTER FOUR

COPING WITH GOD

Bernard J. Bush

Our fourth presentation is entitled, "Coping with God." At first this might seem strange, for it would appear that God has a problem coping with us rather than vice versa. Since coping is adjusting and adapting to the stress caused by change and God is unchanging and unchangeable, we should, it would seem, be able to establish a relationship with Him that does not require coping. Yet, however we explain it, our experience refutes this logic. We certainly are creatures of time and history, of development and growth. That is the way God made us. He has also gone on to reveal Himself as a God of history who is present in and to human affairs. The writer of Hebrews, chapter one, tells us, "at various times in the past and in various different ways, God spoke to our ancestors through the prophets; but in our own time, the last days, He has spoken to us through His Son." This is the image and reality of God with which we must cope. Thus as we progressively discover our own humanity, and the humanity of Jesus, we will find God speaking to us.

The dimension of humanity that is the focal point of these presentations is our adaptive mechanism. We have all known what it is like to be anxious under stress. It is an unwelcome experience for the most part. A great deal of our psychic energy goes into the effort to reduce or eliminate anxiety. Most often anxiety is produced by some change, either external or internal, that we perceive as threatening our safety or well-being. Since our religious beliefs are very near the core of our being, any challenge to change these beliefs will produce feelings of anxiety. Yet within the structures of the Church we find such challenges and changes. When the familiar landmarks of our faith disappear or are discredited, we can feel a kind of disorientation and confusion, if not a sense of outright betrayal. How we handle this anxiety and suffering can tell us a great deal about what kind of persons we are.

ANXIETY

There is a point where anxiety overwhelms us and paralyzes our ability to make creative responses to new situations. There are also degrees of anxiety that are quite healthy and bring us to mobilize the most dynamic energies we have to meet the new challenge. Each person has a different level of tolerance for stress. A situation which causes one person to flourish can cause another to panic. It is important to keep this in mind when we are dealing with ourselves and others. Any teacher can tell us that learning styles and rhythms differ. Some prefer a heavy dose of input with quiet time to assimilate the new experience. Some learn best by taking it gradually and steadily. Some rebel against any challenge to their established beliefs and do not seem to learn or adapt at all. So it is within this context that we have the elements of attitude change, creative adaptation, personal growth, and a spirituality for our times.

I do not think it is an exaggeration to say that until recently spirituality was largely a matter of God up there and me down here. Our salvation was worked out by following the precepts of the Church, the rules of our religious communities, confessing our sins regularly, receiving the Eucharist, and adhering to established devotional practices. We were convinced that if we did these things faithfully we would become holy and save our souls. Community life was devoted to what we used to call edification, a kind of competition for holiness which reduced itself largely to external observance. What we may have been feeling internally was of little interest, attention was directed to development of the will. There was little attempt to work at a happy marriage of faith and feeling. In fact, feelings were considered a positive detriment to sanctity. I remember a popular sarcastic adage about Jesuits which we used to repeat with some pride, "They meet without affection, live in silence, and part without regret." Since the intellectual powers of memory, intellect, and will were considered to be the highest and most noble parts of the soul, we spent years cultivating them. The effect of such training on the emotional lives of many of us was devastating. Somehow what was going on deep inside in the form of anger, love, depression, joy, sorrow, yearning, longing, loneliness, and so forth, did not seem to have much connection to the faith life. In the context of this kind of spiritual bookkeeping, there was an almost constant preoccupation with the state of our souls, adding up the credits and debits with categories such as mortal sin, venial sin and faults against nature. Even after we counted up the balance sheet in an examination of conscience, we were never quite sure what God really thought about us and we would go to confession just to make sure. So the question naturally arises, just what does God think or feel about me? The stage is now set for a form of idolatry.

PROJECTION

Because we are time and earth bound we have a hard time accepting an image of God that is really like God. That is, we tend to make God into our image and likeness. When the question about God's feelings for me arises, the most convenient base for measurement is my own feelings about myself. One of the ordinary mechanisms of defense against anxiety is projection. Projection is attributing to someone else the welcome or unwelcome thoughts and feelings that I have myself. If I am troubled by what I consider to be immoral thoughts, I will tend to attribute immoral motives to the actions of others. I say to myself, "I know what would be on my mind if I were doing that, so it must be on their mind too." I believe that much false religion is projection. The gods of the pagans were largely the projections of the seven deadly sins of humanity. Those gods demanded propitiation for wrongs perpetrated against them. They were capricious, fickle, and unpredictable. The effort to placate them required elaborate expiatory rituals to somehow win their favor or at least buy time from the wrath and fury of these stern, jealous, unloving, relentless gods. Now no one that I know would use these words to describe the God of Abraham, Isaac, Jacob, Jesus, and you and me. Yet do we not often in practice act as if he were like the pagan gods?

These feelings come from within ourselves and are projected outward into the mind of God. We may find that we must punish ourselves mercilessly for real or imagined sins, and even then we will not forgive ourselves. I have seen people who feel as if they are the possessors of the unforgivable sin. Consequently we hold out on our acceptance of other persons until they meet our criteria for acceptable attitudes, dress, mannerisms, actions. It is good to have strong hate for evil actions. Yet have we not all found ourselves at times going beyond this to hate the sinner as well, and feeling quite righteous since we believed that God felt the same way? This is projection. It is the effect of original sin and we all have it. Fortunately, Christ has revealed the real God to us in unmistakably human form, exposed projection for the idolatry that it is, and given us the way to become free from it. It takes a profound conversion to accept the belief that God is tender and loves us just as we are, not in spite of our sins and faults, but with them.

God does not condone or sanction evil, but he does not withhold his love because there is evil in us. The key to this understanding is found in the way we feel about ourselves. We cannot even stand or accept love from another human being when we do not love ourselves, much less believe or accept that God could possibly love us.

Feelings of self-hatred, self-doubt, self-punishment, or guilt arise in that portion of our psyche which classical psychology calls the superego. It is formed early in our childhood by taking in the norms, standards, and values of the authority figures around us. Parents, teachers and religious figures instill their attitudes and judgments when consciousness is being formed. Social and cultural values also play their part. Who can begin to evaluate the impact of that surrogate mother, television, on young minds and hearts? This is a very complex matter, but the point I want to make is that these attitudes and values are formed early, lie very deep within, often beyond consciousness, and are there to be projected outward when we are under stress or when our well-being or even survival seems to be threatened.

In our religious practice there was I believe an unfortunate linkage between the sacraments of Penance and the Eucharist. The impression was often given of trying to polish and shine up the soul so that it would be worthy to enter into the holy of holies; the august presence of God in the Eucharist. I remember being told that Jesus would not like me if I did not go to confession before receiving Holy Communion. Fortunately, this practice is changing, but the old attitudes die slowly when they are deeply ingrained from earliest days. The new liturgical practices mean a new way of thinking about God and ourselves. They are not meant to be the old teaching in a new dress.

GUILT

I would like to speak a bit more about something that I have touched on here and which has been mentioned in the other papers. It is the subject of guilt. There is a great difference between real guilt which is akin to a sense of responsibility based on actually realized freedom of choice, and the feelings of guilt which gnaw at us. The latter feelings are troublesome to deal with, because they can be present when the person has done the objectively right and proper thing. We find in our clinical practice some people who are burdened with guilt, coupled with feelings of insecurity, worthlessness, and depression. These people are generally trying constantly to please others which more often than not brings alienation and rejection rather than the acceptance they so long for. They seem to be completely unable to say "no" to the demands of others. They cannot bring themselves to believe that saying no to the requests and demands of others can in fact be a high form of charity. Religious have been trained to be always and instantly available to the real or imagined needs of everyone but themselves. It is not uncommon to find religious professionals in a state of continual conflict. They feel used, resentful, and depressed when they say yes and overwhelmed with guilt when they even contemplate saying no. If no is said, it is usually the result of two conflicting demands which cannot possibly be met. Humans are limited and cannot be in two places doing two different things at once. But that is not for want of trying! A "yes" does not mean anything unless "no" could just as freely be said. Some people have even made a commitment to religious life because they could not say no to a parent or religious figure they were trying to please by such a step.

I call what I have just been describing the "Avis" spirituality. "We try harder". If anything is going wrong we blame ourselves for not trying hard enough. It is only one step from this to blaming others and scapegoating them, including God, for our own difficulties. This is again the mechanism of projection where one who is motivated by guilt assumes that others are also guilty. At this point I hope it is clear that feelings of guilt, accompanied by anxiety, fear and restlessness, arise from deep within ourselves and are not an accurate gauge of the state of our souls before God. We cannot assume that he feels about us the way we feel about ourselves, unless we love ourselves intensely and freely.

GOD'S REVELATION

Having seen some of the problems with our images of God, I would like now to reflect on God as he has revealed himself to us. When Jesus said that whoever saw him saw the Father, his hearers were shocked beyond belief. These words seem to have lost their shock value to us who have heard them so often. Yet they contain within them all the power to shatter our projections and false images of God. He affirmed that he was the incarnation of all God's thoughts and feelings toward the human race. For us, God is no other than as he is seen in the person of Jesus. The way for this knoweldge was paved by the prophets who relayed God's feelings to us in words we should have been able to understand. God constantly rejected attempts to project our feelings on to him, until finally he sent his Son to convince us. I will simply cite the words of Ezechiel, Chapter 18: "You say, 'The Lord's way is not fair!' Hear now, house of Israel: is it my way that is unfair, or rather, are not your ways unfair? . . . make for yourselves a new heart and a new spirit. . . . I have no pleasure in the death of anyone who dies, says the Lord God. Return and live!"

Jesus, then, has been sent in order that we may live and live abundantly. He is the way, and now through Him, once and for all, the way to God is a human way. The reality that now the way to divinity is through full participation in humanity is truly shocking. It is shocking because it is so inclusive. We are not to factor out parts of our humanity in order to meet God and have a relationship of love with him. He was like us in all things. This includes our feelings, emotions, passions, reactions, limitations, deficiencies, in short, everything we have in common with Jesus. As we come to believe this more, we will come to trust our instincts, and welcome our feelings and reactions. It is acceptable to be angry. Jesus was angry. It is evidence of the Holy Spirit when we have tender passionate feelings. Jesus was a tender man who felt passionately. It is virtuous to change our minds. Jesus changed his mind at times. Who likes to change their mind? This is especially true when the belief is cherished and firmly held. Yet in the scripture there is a beautiful story of a time when Jesus had to change his mind under very personally distressing circumstances. In this story, the Father knew that Jesus had narrowed his horizons and had a dangerously chauvinistic view of his mission. The Father sent a particularly annoying messenger to open Jesus' mind. You are all familiar with the story of the Canaanite woman in Matthew, chapter 15. Let me retell it to you.

The woman came to Jesus with a petition, "Lord, Son of David, have pity on me! My daughter is terribly troubled by a demon." From the start she had two strikes against her in gaining a hearing. First she was a pagan despised by the Jews. Secondly, she was a woman, and no self-respecting man of Jesus' time truly believed that a woman had anything important to say. Add to this the fact that she was an evident nuisance, and we can imagine that Jesus must have been sorely tried. The scripture tells us his reaction. He ignored her. He gave her the silent treatment hoping that she would give up and go away. Sensing his feelings, the disciples grew bold and jumped in, "Get rid of her. She keeps shouting after us." So now we have one of the first examples of the male clerical clubby obtuseness that has plagued the Church ever since. The disciples take their cue from the leader and gang up. Now what chance does the woman have with her problem? This group is all closed up and Jesus is no different than the others. At this point in the story, Jesus goes from silence to defensiveness, with his reply having the ring of guilt and narrow religious parochialism. He said, "My mission is only to the lost sheep of Israel." Then the woman wisely avoids an argument of sterile theological debate. She knows well what she is about and what she wants. She simply restates her request, "Lord, help me!" Now in the typical fashion of such interchanges, Jesus goes from trying to lead her into a debate where he could easily have shown her up, to outright insult. Imagine the delight of the disciples standing around spurring him on. He tells her, "It is not right to take the food of sons and daughters and throw it to the dogs." In a beautiful move, she adds a touch of irony and humor and makes Jesus eat his own words. She does not deny what he said, or get into a defensive angry argument with this obviously prejudiced man. With a deft play on words, she says, "Even the dogs eat the leavings that fall from their masters' tables." At this point, Jesus woke up and had his mind expanded. He realized that he had been on the wrong track. Through this relationship he saw the hand of the Father prodding him to revise his understanding of his mission. A conversion took place in him. Now he could listen to her, truly listen to her, and be able to respond to her in her need and learn something about himself and the Father in the process. When he understood what was really happening, he exclaimed, "Woman, you have great faith! Your wish will come to pass." That very moment her daughter got better.

What I have just given is not the traditional interpretation of that text. The usual explanation is that he was somehow teasing her into greater faith. I choose to take the passage as it stands. This understanding makes a great deal more sense in human terms and certainly makes Jesus more credible. I can identify with a man who does not have the whole picture and must learn and be changed in many different ways. The challenges that are most effective for change in me are the ones that come from human intermediaries, even when they are difficult to hear. Jesus to me then is not the answer man. He is not the one who has nothing to learn from other humans. He is human and in being so, he shares with all of us the need to change. Above all he is honest and willing to admit his mistakes and prejudices. I find these very human qualities in Jesus most endearing and for me they are compelling evidence of the mystery of the human in the divine that is Jesus and in which I also share.

PRAYER

We have been discussing the effect of prayer in the life of Jesus. From his contemplation he was familiar with the ways of the Father and thus he was prepared to recognize him in the daily events of his life. Because he was eminently free he was able to respond to the presence of the Father in whatever way was appropriate. This is rendering true prayer to God. Phrases such as, "I give you thanks, Father," "I praise you, Father," "Not my will, but yours," "Blessed are you, Peter, the Father has revealed this," "Woman, great is your faith," are all prayerful feeling responses to the discerned presence of God speaking to him through others. Contemplation, then, is losing oneself in loving surrender to the awe and wonder of the mystery of another. The surrender of Jesus to the felt presence of the Spirit which he and the Father shared is always appropriate and complete. His whole being goes out until at the end he pours out His entire life in the final act of surrender.

One of the most charming stories of Jesus and his relationships is the one that tells of the time when he was bantering with the attractive Samaritan woman at the well. It is given in John's Gospel, chapter 4. The woman who had had five husbands and was living with a sixth certainly must have had charm which I am sure Jesus noticed and to which he responded. From this story and others it is evident that Jesus enjoyed close and warm relationships with women. Their reputations did not seem to bother him much. He was much more interested in the persons. The reference in the story of the woman at the well to living water welling up from within sounds very much like a description of his own emotional response of love for her. When she inquires further about this living water, he sends her to get her husband. For her, that would be the appropriate source for such living water. He does not seem to be afraid to label his own reactions as the action of the Holy Spirit of Love within himself. He then goes on to speak of prayer and worship saying that authentic worshippers will worship the Father in Spirit and in truth. Again we see him finding the Father in a very human interaction.

Jesus was not afraid to be touched, emotionally and physically, as the Gospel of Luke tells us in chapter 7. There the penitent woman, loving Jesus deeply and emotionally, weeps, perfumes, washes, and embraces him. He accepts and returns the love. The person who is condemned in that scene is the pharisee, Simon, who was afraid to love and sat back judging and projecting his own immoral thoughts and motives onto Jesus. Then in a most amazing statement Jesus glorifies her love by saying, ". . . her many sins are forgiven — because of her great love. Little is forgiven the one whose love is small." This is no abstract love that he is talking about. It is profound, warm, passionate, and sexual. How did Jesus cope with his sexual feelings? He accepted them and found in them occasion to discover the presence of the Holy Spirit in the flesh. We can almost hear the song of praise welling up from within him as he contemplates his own humanity. "It was you who created my inmost self, and put me together in my mother's womb; I give you thanks for all these mysteries, for the wonder of myself, for the wonder of your works". (Ps 139: 13, 14)

LOVE

In none of these encounters do we detect the slightest bit of discomfort in Jesus. He accepts and rejoices in his humanity. He does not label any of his responses or feelings as evil. In fact he declares that expansion of heart in this way increases the capacity to give and receive love, which in turn leads to forgiveness and salvation. If such experiences lead to fear, closing up, constriction of heart and soul, we can suspect the presence of the enemy of humanity, "the accuser of our brother . . . who night and day accuses them before our God." (Rev. 12:10) By contemplating scripture in this way, we can see in the words, responses, and actions of Jesus, the way the Father communicates himself. We can then find him sharing his life with us in the same way.

From what has been said so far, the criteria and norms for our relationship with God will not be the judgments, fears, and guilts that we have within ourselves, but rather the quality of our social relationships. We need only read Matthew, chapter 25, to find confirmation that "as often as you did it for one of my least brothers (and sisters), you did it for me."

The Lord has enjoined on each of us to consider ourselves the least of all. Since whatever is done for the least is done for the Lord, our charity must start with ourselves. In my clinical practice one of the first questions I ask a person is to tell me how he is good to himself. I ask him to be specific. I usually get a look of incomprehension. I then ask him to tell me what he would most like to do — anything goes — use the imagination. It does not even have to be possible. Tell me your impossible dream. In almost every case, this, too, draws a blank. The truth is that most of us who are dedicated religious do not even know how to be good to ourselves. We do not know how to have fun or play. I urge my clients then to set some time aside and let whim be queen for a day. The results for the most part are quite unimaginative. Most often the time is spent visiting friends. These friends frequently turn out to be people with problems that the religious felt compelled to try to help. I hardly call that relaxing recreation or being good to oneself. We religious above all others should live adventurous, creative, exciting and happy lives. Yet tragically it is not so for many.

SIN AND GRACE

It is hard to believe, but sin and grace can be present together in the same person. Imperfection and inspiration are not mutually exclusive. It is one of the many marvels of the teaching and actions of Jesus that gives us this consoling truth. Think of the parable of the weeds and the wheat. Or in a concrete incident, we can remember Peter who was constantly struggling with this reality. One of my favorite examples of this is where Peter in Matthew's Gospel, chapter 16, is the recipient of an inspiration from the Father about the identity of Jesus. Jesus recognized the hand of the Father and affirmed Peter. In the very next moment Peter was listening to another voice which earned him the rebuke, "Get behind me, satan, these are the standards of men, not of God." St. Paul in chapter 7 of his letter to the Romans expresses it agonizingly, "What happens is that I do, not the good I will to do, but the evil I do not intend. What a wretched man I am! Who can free me from this body under the power of death? All praise to God, through Jesus Christ our Lord! So with my mind I serve the law of God but with my flesh the law of sin." It has never been expressed so succinctly. St. Paul can even find the hand of God and a response of praise in the contemplation of his own sinfulness.

CONCLUSION

In conclusion I would like to finish on the one note that I hope has sounded throughout this paper. It is quite simply that God loves us unconditionally. Affective contemplative prayer is our human response to the discovery of God who is everywhere and in and through everything. Humanity is a rich blessing. My hope and prayer is that we will be continually in awe and reverent wonder at its mystery in love.